Apple Wa
For Dumm

Tony Jan

ISBN: 978-1-63750-052-1

Table of content

Introduction

Apple Watch Series 3 is a *Smartwatch* in the Apple lineup. It offers several unique features to make the users more active and better monitor their health among several other great features for humanity. This high-end Smartwatch could be useful for business users, including improved travel notifications and call capabilities.

The Apple Watch looks pretty attractive, right? You must have read and heard about the exciting features like: monitoring your ECG and heartbeat rate, fitness and exercise, location navigation, and many more.

As amazing as all the new features are, it's not quite as easy to use like an iPhone or iPad; the lack of buttons, the smaller screen, and general **UI** can make a frustrating initial experience.

To make things simple, this book has exclusive tips and tasks you can achieve with your new Apple Watch Series. *It also compares the Apple Watch Series 5 to Series 4, and Series 3 here, and that means you can see precisely what the variations and similarities are, whether you are looking to upgrade or take the smartwatch plunge.*

If you are overwhelmed and don't have a lot of time to comb through thousands of tech-pages just to learn how to use an iwatch maximally and effectively, then this book is for you!

In this book, you will learn various tips and tricks such as;

- The differences difference between apple watch series 5, apple watch series 4, and apple watch series 3.
- What's new in WatchOS 6
- How to use iwatch gestures
- Apple Watch ECG monitoring features
- How to sustain battery life
- How to Install the **ECG** and Share ECG Results with your doctor
- How to Setup and Pair Apple Watch with IPhone
- Sending messages and making phone calls
- How to enable fall detection on *iWatch WatchOS 6*
- Adjust Brightness, Sounds, Text Sizes and Haptics on Apple Watch

- Get Notification about Your Friend's Location
- How to use Apple Watch to unlock Mac PC
- How to avoid screen accident with Water lock
- How to control Spotify with Apple Watch
- How to use Apple watch Map to navigate location
- How to update WatchOS
- How to add music to Apple Watch

…and many more!

This book has exclusive tips and in-depth tutorials on the tasks you can achieve with your new Apple Watch Series with the new **WatchOS 6** and **ECG App**. Also; simple enough to understand and a follow-through guide suitable for kids, teens, dummies, and seniors.

This simplified book will also get you equipped with knowledge on how to take the maximum advantage of your *Apple Watch.*

Chapter 1

Apple Watch Guidelines

Ways to get the most from your Smartwatch

If you own an Apple Watch - or you're wondering what Apple's so-called **iWatch** does - you have the very best Smartwatch in the world available. However, there's a steep learning curve and obtaining the most from your Apple Watch and its collection of *fitness, workout, and time-saving features*, which is exactly what this complete guide for Apple Watch is usually to perform.

We've covered the fundamental questions and may support graduate you to a power user - *covering top tips, essential applications, and stylish methods to make your Smartwatch on top.*

What can Apple Watch do?

It's among the typical questions among people thinking about purchasing for the very first time - *what can the Apple Watch do?*

Well, a lot more than just offering you the chance to learn texts and answer calls on your wrist instead of your phone, which will be the primary features everyone understands.

- Obtain emails and notifications around the wrist
- Fitness tracking
- Workout tracking
- Heart rate monitoring
- ECG monitoring (on Watch Series 4 and Series 5 only)
- GPS monitoring of exercises (on GPS variations)
- Make calls and receive communications from your

telephone (LTE variations having a data plan)

- Turn-by-turn navigation
- Siri instructions - alarms, timers, reminders
- Flash seat tickets and boarding passes
- Tell enough time.

Apple Watch Setup

When you take your Apple Watch from the package, it's identical to everyone else's. How come your Smartwatch personal may be the style as well as the apps, this means your Apple Watch will be unique to your preference.

1. Insert your **Apple ID**.

2. Create a passcode.

3. Install your apps.

4. Calibrate your activity configurations.

5. Manage your notifications.

6. Backup your settings.

How to use Apple Watch

The Apple Watch could be tough to split, as well as the first daytime can be viewed as just a little frustrating for the uninitiated. Navigating choices and seeking the information you are thinking about may take a while to get. Though, you'll be using the digital crown, adding and using complications, changing watch faces, and using Apple Pay.

 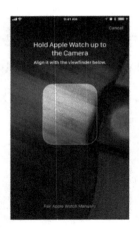 

As you read further, you will be familiar with how to utilize the Apple Watch, including all of the new features and interface tweaks of **WatchOS 6**.

Reset the Apple Watch

The Apple Watch is super secure, so be it lost or stolen, it cannot be used without your permission, this means it needs to be correctly reset and unpaired from your iPhone before it can be added to a brand new one.

For doing that, you need to have a look at your Watch application on your own iPhone and initiate the unpairing procedure.

The Most Effective Apple Watch apps

If there's one major differentiator in the middle of your Apple Watch and any rival, it's the wide breadth of apps, similar to the iPhone. Apple has remained the killer top features of the Apple Watch up to its developers.

Top Apple Watch application picks

- *Strava*

- *Spotify*

- *Espn*

- *Carrot Fit*

- *Streaks*

- *Autosleep*

- *Simply Press Record*

- *Citymapper*

··· among numerous others based on your preferred functions.

Chapter 2

Apple Watch Activity and Workout

Among the top features of the Apple Watch, will be as a *fitness tracker and athletics watch*. The sweetness from the Smartwatch is usually adding this sort of features right into a unitary device - despite the fact that it's taken some time, the Apple Watch is a significantly powerful device.

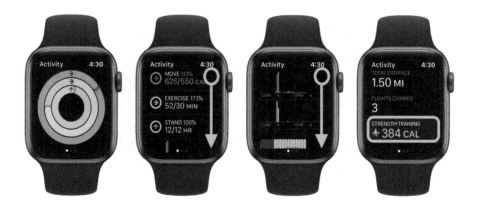

Apple Watch: Fitness and Activity Explained

It's an excellent fitness tracker and may also monitor routines - and when you have a string 5 with Navigation, it can replace your standard fitness watch. The experience application monitors motion, calories burned, and standing time. And you're encouraged to 'close the bands' to create your day-by-day goals.

Gleam Breathe app, which stimulates mindfulness, and taking periods of your mood. All stats are viewable around the Watch, are monitored within the knowledge application on your own iPhone, and populate the Apple Health app, too.

Apple Watch: Workout Application

The Workout application is a different beast and gives you to track several different activities, from running and cycling to indoor workouts (which essentially track your heart rate, calories, and time spent).

The Workout application now features:

- *Indoor Walk.*

- *Outdoor Walk.*

- *Indoor Run.*

- *Outdoor Run.*

- *Indoor Cycle.*

- *Outdoor Cycle.*

- *Elliptical.*

- *Rower.*

- *Pool Swim.*

- *Open drinking water Swim.*

- *Yoga.*

- *Hiking.*

Outdoor exercises are tracked with **GPS**, as the other features; *time, heart rate, calories burnt, and a lap characteristic.* They are kept in the knowledge application on your iPhone to find out.

The Workout application was treated to another overhaul in watchO5, with automated run recognition added along with running specific additions such as Speed Alerts and cadence tracking, unlike many sports watches.

Apple Watch ECG Monitoring

Arguably, the biggest addition taken up to the Apple Watch Series 4 (and in addition obtainable in the Series 5) was the *ECG monitor*; it'll track the tempo of the heart, looking for indicators of a-fib (*Atrial fibrillation*) - a problem that is clearly a leading cause of strokes because of poor blood circulation in human. Essentially, it's capable of taking medical-grade readings of the heartbeat, checking for irregular activity as well as letting you possess a PDF accountable to show a medical doctor.

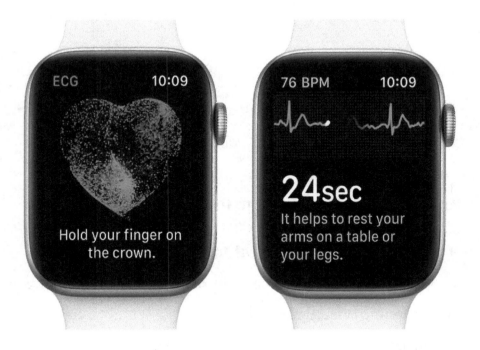

Apple Watch Heart Rate Monitoring

What makes Apple Watch monitor heart rate?

Heart rate monitoring continues to be an essential section of the **Apple Watch**, and because the manufacturing **WatchOS 4** that it's been converted into a robust tool; also; the Apple Watch can utilize your heart rate in the following ways:

- Tracking sleeping heart rate.

- Taking live heart rate readings.

- Tracking heart rate during exercises and deploying

it to provide even more accurate calorie burn.

- Alert user to abnormal or elevated heart rate.

- ECG readings (Apple Watch Series 4 and Series 5 only).

Heart rate activity happens to be tracked throughout the day, and you may also track the heart rate while sleeping, which is a huge indicator of enhancing fitness, as well as fatigue and stress. Also, the heart rate monitor could keep tabs on your ticker and alert you to an elevated **bpm** that may be dangerous.

Chapter 3

Apple Watch Exclusive Features

1. Measure surface angles

Apple Watch Series 5 includes a compass sensor. The same as on iPhone, the Compass application takes to reap the benefits of it for a good level feature. Just scroll down in the application form to gain access to this tool, then layout your Watch on any surface to measure both its horizontal and vertical levels.

2. Enhanced directions in Maps

Like on iPhone, Apple Maps uses the built-in compass sensor to stage the road you're currently facing, that may be found in handy whenever using step-by-step directions.

3. Encompass private stuff with all the current always-on display

The largest fresh feature of Series 5 is its always-on screen that allows you to tell time discreetly and appearance into other information shown around the watch face while inside a gathering or training and never having to flip over your wrist. Fortunately, you may decide to cover any delicate info from your prying eye whenever your wrist is down.

Start by firing in the Watch application on your own iPhone, then tap **My Watch** → **Lighting & Wording Size** → **Always On** and turn the toggle **Cover Sensitive Problems** towards the **OFF** position. *Carrying this out will conceal any issues that screen private data whenever your wrist is down, including Calendar visits, Mail messages, plus your heart rate.*

4. Delete indigenous apps

WatchOS lets you delete stock applications from the home screen, much like **iOS** devices. Let's pretend you'd prefer to eradicate Apple's stock Information app - touch and keep its icon on the home screen, then strike **"x"** and verify the action by tapping ***Delete App***. Don't worry; you can redownload erased stock applications by searching to them in App Store.

5. Utilize dual the storage

Apple Watch Series 5 doubles the inner storage on the predecessors from 16 to 32 gigabytes. Letting you retain more content on the unit itself, from applications to your selected photos to Apple Music playlists, songs and albums, and beyond. This comes into play if you don't possess an LTE watch, so streaming via cellular isn't an option.

6. Reorder your Watch Faces

Like before, you can even edit watch faces within the Watch itself or via the Watch application on your own iPhone, But now, **WatchOS 6** also lets you reorder these to your liking - press and contain the watch face to enter Edit mode, then drag the watch face to a fresh position. It'll be there next time you swipe through your Watch faces.

7. Select any band you want

Finally, you forget about being confined to Apple's mixtures of Apple Watch bands and case materials. With Apple Watch Series 5, you can mix and match bands and case materials in any manner you prefer, whether waiting for you or online.

8. Noise app

Be sure to see the Noise application (and put a Noise complication on your preferred watch face) if you'd choose to exist alerted about connection with noise levels that can harm your hearing. This feature may decrease battery life, so put it to use sparingly, and only one time it's wise (as with, you don't need a Noise complication on your night-time watch face).

9. Track your heart function

Much like Series 3, and series 4, Series 5 includes an electrocardiogram that could keep your life by spotting adverse heart rate results even if you're unacquainted with them, such as whenever your heart rate is accelerating a good deal while you're definitely not doing anything challenging.

10. Finding iPhone at night

That's an oldie, but Goldie. Once you discuss the *Control Center* and tap calling icon, the Watch will ping your misplaced iPhone via Bluetooth or Wi-Fi. But if you touch and keep that same *Control Center* toggle, carrying this out shall produce your telephone flash. That's relatively great when you have no thought where your telephone is or want to think it is at night!

Chapter 4

Incredible actions you can take with Apple Watch Series 5

Apple creator Steve Jobs didn't wear a wristwatch, and according to an interview with Jony Ive (Apple's previous Chief Design Standard), the idea for creating their initial wearable, didn't even happen until 2012. However, Apple loves and appreciates watches and, with each iteration, just like the fresh Apple Watch Series 5, spent a while working to produce it the best-selling wearable watch.

- **Standalone Friend**

It's really worth reiterating that this Apple Watch Series 5 can be an excellent stand-alone digital friend; they have built-in GPS, so you constantly know where you're heading, there is also a 32GB storage for your music, integrated Apple Pay, and, with regards to the model, mobile service for calls, wording, and data (this usually costs approximately $12 monthly extra on your mobile expenses).

Talking about heading it alone, Apple Watch now has immediate usage of the App Store around the Watch; this feature wasn't available during screening, since it will exist when released with **watchOS 6**, meaning other Apple Watch models may also access the store.

Integrated with health monitoring is Apple Watch's heart rate monitor; consequently, I always know what sort of exercise, relaxing, and recovery heart rates I'm attaining. It is also viewing for abnormal and high heart rates, and there's an integral electrocardiogram and **ECG App**. To make use of it, I make certain the Watch is snug on my wrist, and after 30 secs, I understand easily possess sinus tempo (sound) or have to visit a doctor.

- *Apple Watch Series 5* is always ready for a swim, and so is created for a gentle browse in about up to 50M of drinking water. The Apple Watch Series 5 I tested, a 44 mm stainless model having a Milanese loop group and cellular support, costs $799; nevertheless, you can buy a 38mm GPS-only model using a sports group for under $399.

Cellular connectivity is usually nice to have, as would be the high-end materials, but I really believe the 38mm Apple Watch Series 5 is an excellent value, so you even now get the Always-On flash, map access, the compass and everything medical and activity features. Apple Watch Series 5 doesn't invariably improve the pub for smartwatches but, with it, Apple has polished the already excellent wearable. I remain a fan.

- **Sustaining Battery Life**

Keeping the flash on all the time naturally means the Apple Watch screen uses more battery life, but Apple mixed the **LTPO** *(Low-temperature poly-silicon and oxide)* tech with a brand new low-power screen driver, and even more energy-efficient force management integrated circuit, and a far more ambient light sensor.

An edge of keeping the *Apple Watch Series 5* from growing to be a power-draining device is by maintaining it inside a darkened theatre or supper spot; the sensor can pay better concentrate on its light environment, and I remarked that it actually muted the screen brightness in my living room where I'd dimmed the lamps to view

Television.

I've gotten familiar with the sometimes-over-bright Apple Watch face when I first glanced in the now more tactful interface; We used to be straining just a little to see it; that is "my" problem, not "Apple Watch" problem. It wasn't quite a while before I acquired utilized to the reactive Apple Watch Series 5 screen, I likewise own the decision of increasing the default flash screen brightness. However, that may adversely impact my battery pack strength.

However, Apple will flourish in your time and effort to create an always-on screen in an Apple Watch that lasts 18 hours a comparable charge. I've worn the Apple Watch Series 5 all day every day without ever operating out of power before setting it again within the wireless charging during the night.

- **Time for the one Big Change**

The Apple Watch Series 5 framework hasn't changed out in this past year, except the Always-On Retina Screen, which includes being the Apple Watch Series 5's most crucial change; however, Apple Watch OS 6 offers plenty of valuable improvements, but keeps up with the same design.

Apple Watch ensure almost 18-hours of smartwatch battery pack life, but when We lower the wrist, the Watch became an inert little metallic having a dark cup (or sapphire crystal) face. The Always-On screen isn't just a "leave it on and hope battery life isn't terrible technology." I really like how Apple thought this through the use of an assortment of technologies to keep carefully the face lit and glanceable no matter what.

Recently, Apple introduced **LPTO** *(Low-temperature poly-silicon and oxide)* technology to its **OLED** Retina flash within its bigger flash (in addition, it curved the corners).

It's **LTPO** *(Low-temperature poly-silicon and oxide)* that allows the Apple Watch Series 5 to decelerate its refresh rate from **60 Hz** to at least **1 Hz** (basically from 60 times per second to one or more times per second), this provides you with it a much slower and less power consuming screen refresh rate. As a result of this, the flash will still only change for a meeting or crucial notification or only one time every minute. Concerning the Infograph watch face that always includes a second-hand cruising for the facial skin since it ticks off a couple of seconds, the next hands disappear in the Always-On setting in support of adjustments at minute intervals.

The greater apparent change in "Constantly On" mode will be the white-coloured backgrounds turn black on some faces. In others, bright colours go more muted. Apple modified all its Watch encounters to work in Always On setting. Overall, the lighting diminishes using what is approximately 50 percent, and the result is usually a wristwatch face that is relaxing but could be read despite the fact that I glance down in my wrist.

- **Shows You Direction**

As I mentioned, one of the better Apple Watch features is its navigational features, driven by *Apple Maps*; the application form is usually installed in the Watch and may inform me exactly which path I'm facing. An individual interface is comparable to a physical compass in digital form, and swiping through; the interface provides my using even more specific location details, including latitude, longitude, and floor elevation. I didn't experience the opportunity to climb any mountains, but, predicated on the Apple Watch Series 5 compass, I'm at about 20 feet above sea level in my home and, on the 8th floor of my office, about 80 foot above sea level. Usage of this detail flash helps it feels like I've tapped right into a primary hand out from your Apple Watch Series 5 detectors.

We liked the compass a whole lot that I added, and it offers little details of more information on the wristwatch face, just like the period or your sessions) on my go-to watch face. Nobody will ever be capable to stage me in the wrong direction again. There are a couple of additional exciting updates on Apple Watch Series 5; Siri now has Shazam-like features (while I pay attention to music, I possibly could lift my hands and have Siri, "What's that track?"), the Smartwatch uses its mics to give consideration, and it correctly recognizes songs, even showing album covers.

Siri may also search the web and flash a listing of *SERPs*

over the Watch, so once I obtain the administrative centre of Texas, I acquired a perfect effect (it's Austin). However, once I asked Siri, showing me iPhone reviews, she told go surfing to find more information about iPhone.

- **Security and More**

There are a number of fresh safety features that are extremely difficult for me to test. The very best is usually Sound; it could show you the existing ambient sound level in decibels, and if the long-term usage of it'll harm your hearing. You can also set up the Apple Watch Series 5 to warn you if you're in times (for many minutes) with ear-drum-damaging sound levels.

There's also the ability to help to make International crisis/emergency calls through the Watch in over 150 countries. Appears to be a great characteristic I hope never to usage.

Top Features of Apple Watch Series 5

An excellent move is to change things less than it is possible to, and lean into what folks like, and fix small, petty issues yourself. Externally, the apple watch series 5 gets the same size and form as the Apple Watch Series 4, but Apple has made a small number of adjustments which current (and future) Apple Watch followers will value, as the utmost apparent may be the always-on screen.

I've been using Apple Watches for a long period, and so far as I like them, I never knew I'd so fall deeply in love with the brand new feature of me reducing my arm, as well as the screen goes completely dark. Real watches never pull the plug on, also digital ones.

- **Select Your Design**

I never had a problem with Apple offering matched pairings from the Apple Watch and group, but many people thought they needed more options. An attribute Apple calls Apple Studio room, which lets you select your Apple Watch materials and bands individually for an authentic mix-and-match experience.

Also, it's really worth noting as the Apple Watch starts at $399 (GPS, only), it is possible to wind up by choosing stainless, brushed titanium (which is lighter yet more powerful than stainless), and even ceramic (which is gorgeous). If you want the option from the $199 Apple Watch, you'll have to return the still-available Series 3. It's an excellent product but won't feature a compass or the brand new always-on screen feature.

Which Way to visit?

Being truly a directionally challenged person, I'm probably more excited about the Apple Watch Series 5's new compass features and application than I am. I really like it when my Watch can inform me not merely the path from the North Pole but through the north. The Apple Watch changes for seasonal variants from the poles; therefore, you don't obtain "sort of" north; you get genuine. The application itself is usually smooth and worked flawlessly in the demonstration space. I scrolled to the Compass App flash screen and observed also, it shows a sea-level altitude reading.

Certainly, the compass will be a lot even more useful when it's built-into other apps, like Apple's maps app. Now the Apple Watch map screen could have the same "which way am I facing" arrow as it could around the iPhone. Furthermore, third-party companies, like Yelp, can integrate the same arrow, so you know which way to discover that astonishing Thai restaurant.

Apple didn't execute a good deal using the Apple Watch Series 5 security features but did put the energy for the cellular types from the Apple Watch to dial crisis services (think 911 in the U.S. or 112 in Spain) in 150 different countries. So, when there is a fall in China, the Watch can identify it and call municipality bodies.

- **This Watch Screen is Always On**

The Apple Watch Series 5 flash screen, automatically switches from full lighting and color to a comparatively dimmer light when you decrease your wrist. What you'll then see is a mainly black background screen with lighter colors for elements you'd want to see; when you increase your wrist, the screen changes back to full color.

Behind the scenes is definitely something called low heat polysilicon and oxide (**LTPO**) screen; in Always-On Setting, the **LPTO** changes the flash screen refresh rate from an even more power starving 60 Hz to at least one 1

Hz; as a result of this, the low-power always-on flash will, for instance, just change once every second. When the always-on flash screen feature is enabled, it removes most of the white-color from most Apple Watch faces, nonetheless, it doesn't remove complications; those features still arrive, though they upgrade within the second-by-second basis.

When I tried the brand-new flash in the demonstration space, I have been surprised at how well the flash screen switched from active mode to always-on mode by simply raising and lowering my hands. Apple also addressed among my various other Apple Watch frustrations: the too-bright flash in the darkroom; now, the ambient light sensor is continually scanning for different light situations, and you'll be much dimmer within a cinema than it could be outside.

Chapter 5

How to Use the Apple Watch Maximally

When the Apple Watch arrived in 2015, it wasn't merely a new product: it was Apple's first entry into wearables, a completely new market it had previously shied from. Unfortunately, without interface custom to attract on, this managed to get very hard for Apple to attain the same degrees of user-friendliness it experienced using its **Macs and iOS devices.**

Instead, Apple forged a new design program. You would find multiple control methods - a touch screen that's delicate to two examples of pressure, a button and a dial, and tone of voice control - and numerous third-party applications that take different methods to a user interface that took a couple of years to stay down; this means *Apple Watch* is filled with crucial features and unknown potential. In this book, you will learn tips and secrets to get more out of your Watch, from essential interface ways to obscure tips for optimizing how applications behave. And up-to-date regularly to include new features added in *WatchOS software* improvements.

Utilize the Digital Crown to Navigate

When people first began to use the Apple Watch, they found themselves wanting a Home button like the main one below the flash screen on the iPhone and iPad. But there's already a home button: The Digital Crown. Pressing the **Digital Crown** performs activities like the Home button on your iPhone: touch it once to return to the house flash or press and keep it to activate Siri.

Digital Crown/
Home button

Side button

Although there is not much in the form of multitasking on the Apple Watch, the **Digital Crown** can also allow something similar.

If you are using the Apple Watch and want to go back to the last application that was used quickly, double-tap the Digital Crown, and the last application will be opened automatically. (This also works from the clock face.) Then, once you're completed using that app, you can change back to the first app (which is currently the 'last-used app') by again double-pressing the Digital Crown.

Utilize the Digital Crown to open up Apps

There are a variety of methods for you to navigate around the Apple Watch. You merely have to get the way that is right for you; for example, applications on the Home menu can be opened up by tapping the icon, but many people have discovered that tapping is inaccurate; sometimes you miss and open up the app left or right of your desired app.

To get the application in a crowded home flash screen, you may want to focus away using the Digital Crown to get the desired app. Once you have located it, tap near it to move on the region, and then centre the application on the flash.

Once it's centered, rather than tapping it, use the Digital Crown to focus it and open up it - it's a lot more accurate and carries a cool computer animation when zooming in to the watch face. On the other hand, try the alphabetical List View rather than the Grid View - this is simpler to navigate. Perform a hard-press on the home menu and select the appropriate option.

Use (Customize) the Application Dock

The simplest way to open an application on your Watch - or a popular app, at the very least - is to apply the dock that was added with **WatchOS 3** and redesigned in WatchOS 4. This fast-launching application picker is accessed by pressing the medial side button.

Any application can reside in the dock, whether or not it's pre-installed or created by an authorized user. Apps you place there are constantly refreshed, and that means you can easily see a live preview when you swipe laterally in the dock. Tapping on an application from its live preview will open it instantly.

You can choose up to 10 applications to put in the dock.

Open up the Apple Watch application on your iPhone, then tap *My Watch > Dock*. Make sure favourites are ticked at the very top, then tap the *Edit* option at the top to move applications into or from the dock. You can even choose which order they come in. Additionally, tick Recent and WatchOS would automatically populate the dock with the applications you've been using lately.

Keep Tab on Control Centre

Swiping through to the watch face discloses Control Centre. You will see how much electric battery strength you have used; touch the percentage physique for quick access to Power Reserve if you want to conserve it.

There's also Airplane Mode, Cinema Setting (indicated by two masks - this stops the flash screen), silent mode, Do Not Disturb, a torch, a ping button for locating your phone, and an **AirPlay** button for hearing music from your Apple Watch with wireless headsets or a Bluetooth loudspeaker, and if you are utilizing a waterproof model (Series 2 or later) you will see water lock too, indicated with a droplet icon; this converts off the touch screen so that it isn't triggered by moving water in the shower or pool.

Improve Battery Life

How is your Watch's electric battery performing? The initial and Series 1, when brand-new, could make it through one day's moderate use fairly easily: with careful use, they will make it through the majority of another as well.

Series 2, the best electric battery performer up till now, was best for two times useful between charges, and we discovered that it frequently managed to get to lunchtime on the third.

Series 3 and Series 4 have been similar to one. Five to two times, although they rely heavily on how much you utilize cellular, which really is a battery killer.

If you are not getting these degrees of performance - and understand that electric battery life is one of the things that suffers most as a tool age - then it's well worth phoning Apple Support to find out if you have a duff model. But there are a few simple tricks you can test first.

It's possible that you need to check your use of precise, particularly power-hungry apps. Some watch consumes more power than others; some configurations are better for enhancing battery life. Reducing notifications - and motivating your Watch to check on, is using its combined iPhone for improvements less often - are well worth a try.

Walkie-Talkie

This application was added within the WatchOS 5 updates, and we enjoy it - although we're yet to be convinced that it is a particularly practical feature. Still, it's free, and for that reason, worth checking out for fun only. Open up the Walkie-Talkie application, and you'll see a list of individuals you can speak to. Touch the plus indication in the bottom to include more.

Now, from the app's main user interface screen, touch one of the yellow contact symbols to start speaking with them. Assuming they provide authorization (a one-off necessity), you can share instantly. Keep down the Chat button to chat; release to listen.

Don't run out of Data

If you have bought the cellular-equipped version of the Apple Watch Series 3 or Series 4, you do not simply need to be concerned about the electric battery working out. Additionally, you need to take into account your computer data limit.

You will keep a record of your computer data use and limit by logging into the **EE account** online or utilizing the **My EE** application for mobile. The application has one section for the phone and another for the Watch. Many Apple Watch apps, both first- and third-party, will offer you ways to limit data utilization. Check carefully to see what your options are for the applications you prefer, and consider tensing data usage.

Finally, like the majority of streaming services, Apple Music runs on a lot of data. If you are approaching your regular monthly data limit, this can be a good application to stay away from.

Select a New Watch Face

Apple introduced three new watch encounters in

WatchOS 3: Numerals, a stunningly simple face with clock hands and, you guessed it, numerals; Activity, which places your rings front side and center on the screen in either analogue or digital form; and Minnie Mouse to become listed on her pal Mickey. Various Toy Tale character types joined the team in WatchOS 4, along with a stylish rotatable kaleidoscope face, while WatchOS 5 added cool fire and liquid metal effects.

To add new encounters to your line-up, open up the Watch application on your iPhone and tap on Face Gallery underneath navigation pane. You can transform the order that will show up by tapping the **Edit** button next to *My Watch > My Encounters*.

You can customize that person (including its colours and complexions), or you can swipe from left to right either left or directly on the watch screen to see more faces in the order you selected above.

Avoid Accidentally Changing the Watch Face

We've noticed from some individuals who find that they unintentionally change watch face without indication;

this happens mostly in the shower, where, in fact, the warm water will often trick the Watch into thinking it's being touched with a fingertip, with the effect that you emerge from the shower with lots of settings - perhaps like the selection of watch face - inadvertently changed.

But it is also easy to mistakenly swipe to a fresh face with all the touch screen for other activities.

If you're an exceptional shower personalized being, the perfect solution is easy: start water Lock, this briefly deactivates the touch screen and therefore prevents functions or configurations being messed with by the meddlesome water, but if you merely use one face and would prefer not to need the watch change to others in error, you may as well delete all others from your "My Encounters list."

Open up the Watch application on your iPhone and, in the **My Watch** tabs, touch on **Edit** next to **My Encounters**. Touch the red group next to the unwanted encounters, then tap **Done**. They're not gone forever - you can go into the Face Gallery anytime to retrieve them.

Rename Your Apple Watch

In case your name is David, for instance, and someone happens to obtain two Apple Watches, and you choose to keep these things both paired to the same iPhone at the same time, you might find yourself in the annoying situation of being unsure of which "David's Apple Watch" is which. Not that we're speaking from experience or anything.

One solution is by using a different face on each Watch, but if you'd like to keep your favourite on both, a much better solution is to rename one of the watches to "David's Apple Watch Series 2" or "Watchy Mc Watch face."

Renaming your Apple Watch is simply knowing how the option is strangely well concealed. Open up the Watch application on your iPhone, make sure you're in the **My Watch** tabs, then touch **General > About > Name** and *enter a fresh name*, then tap **Done**.

Avoid Screen Accidents with Water Lock

For Apple Watch Series 2 And Later Only.

As briefly discussed already, water Lock is a fresh feature, added in watchOS 3 with the improved water-resistance of the Apple Watch Series 2 at heart. It is rather handy (and turned on automatically) when you set to plan swimming regularly in the Workout app, but it is also smart to transform it by hand in the shower.

Swipe up from underneath of the flash to share the Control Centre, with a variety of popular controls. Tap the tiny water droplet icon.

To turn **Water lock** off again, rotate the Digital Crown dial. Water Lock will be deactivated, and you will hear a sound – i.e., the loudspeaker vibrating to drive out any remaining water. Water Lock is fired up automatically if you go to **workout app**. But if you begin another workout – such as running - and then it begins to rain greatly, you can activate the feature from within the Workout app. Swipe in from the still left, and you'll start to see the typical options to pause or stop the workout, but there may also be a droplet icon to turn on water

Lock carefully. The workout will continue; however, the touchscreen will be desensitized, so you will have to rotate the dial before using any onscreen functions.

We've never encountered rain sufficiently heavy to activate the Watch's flash screen, but we do often utilize this feature whenever we run while wearing a jacket; it halts the sleeve from unintentionally pausing the workout, changing application or worse.

Change volume on AirPods

If you open up the *Now Playing* application on your Apple Watch while using a set of AirPods, you can transform the volume using the Digital Crown dial.

To open up *Now Playing*, touch the media side button, swipe to the right face, and tap the application. If it's not in the dock, you can transform this by starting the Watch application on the companion iPhone and heading to *My Watch > Dock*.

Better still, with certain types of Watch, it is possible to change the volume of the AirPods even if the flash is off. Open up the *Now Playing app*, then allow screen dim, and you will find you can change the dial and change the volume without activating increase to wake.

Practise Mindfulness with Breathe

watchOS 3 brought with it a new built-in application called Breathe. Its purpose is mindfulness: the application was created to show you through sleep classes, so you'll give more consideration to your mental health, which frequently gets the brief end of the stay when discussing wellness; you can as well customize this app on the Watch application, just pair your iPhone. Make sure you're in the *My Watch* tabs and then scroll down and touch *Breathe*; from here, you can pick how often you want reminders to breathe each day (or switch off notifications entirely) and just how many breaths each minute is preferred. You can even adapt *Breathe's haptics*, the vibrations that will walk you through each session.

Apple's watchOS 5 series added a *Breathe watch face*, which you can access from the *facial Gallery* in the Watch application on iPhone. Tap to edit, and you could select from the traditional style, or new Quiet and Focus variations.

Use your iPhone to unlock your Apple Watch

Whenever you placed on your Apple Watch, you're prompted to enter your passcode to get access. Granted, it generally does not take lengthy time to tap in your passcode, but some individuals think it is fiddly, especially if you have one of the smaller-screen models. Fortunately, you have time to get accustomed to the workaround (I don't mean disabling the passcode, making things easier for thieves).

When you at first create your Apple Watch, you were asked whether you wished to unlock it, making use of your iPhone. If you have chosen yes, unlock your iPhone if you are prompted for your Apple Watch security password, and it will unlock your Watch too. The procedure is manufactured even easier with *Touch ID* or *Face ID*.

If you didn't allow the setting at first but want to now, open up the Watch application on your iPhone and demand Passcode menu, from here, all you have to do is toggle the *'Unlock with iPhone'* option.

Use your Apple Watch to unlock your Mac

Apple's synchronicity between the devices arrived to play with watchOS 3 and macOS Sierra. Now you can use your Apple Watch to unlock your Mac computer, no security password necessary. First, ensure that your Macintosh and Apple Watch are both authorized into the same iCloud accounts and allow a passcode on your Watch if you haven't already. On your own Mac computer, click through the following configurations: *System Settings > Security & Personal privacy > General.* Enable *'Allow your Apple Watch to unlock your Macintosh.'*

When you have two-step confirmation turned on, you will have to change to two-factor authentication instead, otherwise, you will discover yourself jogging into a wall structure of frustration. You can view which security method you're using by putting your signature on the *Apple ID* accounts.

To carefully turn off two-step verification and allow two-factor authentication, follow Apple's user guide.

How to Take Screenshots with an Apple Watch

Going for a screenshot on Apple Watch - taking a static image of whatever's on the flash at confirmed moment, quite simply, which means you can share it or save it for future research. You can press the medial side Button and the Digital Crown at the same time, and the screenshot would pop-up in the Photos application on the matched iPhone, but because the start of iOS 10 and watchOS 3, Apple Watch screenshots have been handicapped by default.

If you wish to re-enable screenshots, open up the Watch application on the paired iPhone and tap **General**. Scroll down again and tap the slider next to allow Screenshots so that it turns *green*.

Now you can use the old technique: press the medial side button and Digital Crown at the same time, then try looking in Photos on the iPhone for the screenshot.

Use Your Apple Watch to hit Your Fitness Targets

The *Activity app*, as its name suggests, tracks your exercise: the more you maneuver around, the more you increase your heart rate, and the less you take a seat on your bum, the better your progress towards three daily targets.

If you are finding it hard achieving your *fitness target*, you can always lower the prospective - it is the only one of the three that is user-customizable. If you are in the *activity app*, execute a company press on the flash screen, and you'll start to see the option to improve *Fitness Goal*; this will connect with today's target, and that means you can always lower the target in an 'about to lose out on an accomplishment' emergency. After all adjusting your targets - there are many ways to burn off through those last few calorie consumptions before you go out of time. Most importantly, don't assume you must do a full-on workout or even go outside.

Relatively static activities could work quite effectively, so long as you're active just a little and getting the heart going - we find practicing forward-defensives with a child's cricket bat curiously effective, presumably since it involves steps ahead, back, and exercising many areas of the body. Conversely, doing the football mini-game on Wii Sports activities seems much less effective, presumably because our foot hardly moves.

Jogging at that moment, provided it's reasonably vigorous running at that moment, happens to be our go-to approach topping up unburned calories by the end of your day; for the Stand total, be aware that just standing up for one minute isn't enough going to the mark for just about any given hour. You will need to go around just a little for the Watch to note; walking right down to your kitchen and making a glass of tea should be enough, but there is that when cushioning across the house in socks or house slippers (especially on carpet), it sometimes does not grab the steps or challenges to choose it up for some time.

If you are desperate going to the mark, you could put shoes on or go and walk in your kitchen or jump along for a bit, but make an effort to understand that by sitting less, you see medical benefits whether you win the 'game' or not.

Share your Activity rings

Activity-sharing on the Apple Watch gives you to see your friends' daily improvement in conference to their activity goals, from workout details with their rings. You can send positive messages to encourage a pal who requires a boost from the watch Activity app, or if you are feeling competitive, some prewritten snark is only a tap away.

Activity-sharing isn't fired up by default: you have to invite friends to share their data with you and await them to reply, i.e., in the iOS Activity app, not the iOS Apple Watch app - select the Posting tab underneath, then touch the + signal at top right. Enter a contact address, or search your contacts, then choose **Send**. They'll have to accept simply. If you are feeling particularly competitive (and also have updated to WatchOS 5 or later), you can also challenge your pals to a competition.

Take Photos with Your Apple Watch

Apple pre-installs a Camera application with the Apple Watch. That may seem unusual because no available

Apple Watch model includes a camera of any sort; this app allows you to use the Watch as a remote control shutter result in your iPhone camera; it's a useful feature to have.

Open up the Camera application on your Apple Watch, and it'll automatically open up the Camera application on the paired iPhone.

Start the timer.

Take a photo.

Prop up the iPhone in a good vantage point (perhaps use one of the lovely iPhone camera tripods?) while looking at the shot is directly on your Apple Watch. If you are happy, you can touch the white group on the watch flash to have a picture or strike the '3s' button to employ a three-second delay.

Make your iPhone Flash when Pinging it

Now, this may be two tips for Apple Watch users that weren't already alert to a Find my iPhone style 'Ping,' that you can activate to find your iPhone. If you are at home and can't find your iPhone anywhere (we've all been there), you can merely gain access to the Settings Glance from your Apple Watch and tap the iPhone icon at the bottom of the flash screen; this will send a sign to your iPhone and make it 'ping' loudly, letting you easily think it is.

A convenient feature to have, right? But if you cannot find your iPhone by pinging it alone, touch and maintain the ping iPhone icon on your Apple Watch to activate the cameras LED flash as well, that may hopefully offer you a better notion of where your missing device is.

Dismiss Notifications without removing them from Notification Centre

When you get a notification on your iPhone, it's flashed on your Apple Watch - certainly. But did you see that once a notification has been dismissed on your Apple Watch, it is also dismissed from your iPhone's notification centre? Although it means you will keep your Notification Centre from becoming too cluttered, additionally, it may come as a drawback in relation to message notifications.

Say, for example, I get a *WhatsApp message notification* on my Apple Watch from my pal while I'm at work and can't answer him immediately. Easily dismiss the notification from my Apple Watch; it'll also dismiss it from my iPhone - however, in doing this, I completely ignore that he has messaged me, and I finish up disregarding his message all night. Not ideal, could it be?

There's a straightforward workaround available, though - whenever you've received a complete screen notification you don't want to dismiss from the notification centre, press the Digital Crown to come back from what you were doing without removing it.

Quickly Clear all Notifications

If you follow our previous advice regarding not dismissing notifications on your Apple Watch, one side-effect may be a big volume of notifications in your Apple Watch Notification Centre, available by swiping down from the watch face. Although we may not need to clear important communications/notifications, we don't want you to drown in a sea of irritating notifications either.

When you are in times like the main one described above, there are two possibilities for you: manually clear each notification by swiping left onto it and tapping *'Clear,'* or *clear all notifications* simultaneously. To clear all of your notifications simultaneously, gain access to the *Notification Centre*, and tap *Clear All*; this will clear all notifications from both your ***Apple Watch*** *and* ***iPhone***.

. Let Shazam tell you all the music it heard today

Apple depends on developers to generate alternative

third-party apps to help make the Apple Watch experience as high as possible, and that's what the actual programmers of **Shazam** did. Just how many moments are you on trips and noticed a song that you want, but weren't sure what it was called? **Shazam** gives you the identification of the track you can hear right from your wrist - but that isn't all it can do.

From within the **Shazam** for Apple Watch app, force touch to share about a fresh menu. From here, you can select *"Start Auto Shazam"* that will constantly pay attention to your environment and identify any tracks that you hear as you start your entire day. Then, it curates that music into a playlist in Shazam; after that, you can export into Spotify.

Control Spotify using Your Apple Watch

The Music application for the Apple Watch is impressive, providing you full usage of your complete iPhone music library and permitting you to browse by song, artist, album, etc. However, imagine if, like us, you do not use the stock Music application on your iPhone and instead use a third-party option like **Spotify**? There are still ways to get (limited) control of your music via the **Apple Watch**.

Instead of starting the Music application to gain access and control the music stored on your iPhone, first open up Spotify or any other very good music player on your iPhone and begin playing music. Once music is playing, press the medial side button on your Apple Watch to open up the dock and see *"Now Playing."* It appears similar to the Music app but gives you to regulate the music that's playing no matter where it's from.

You can pause, play, forward and back, and control the volume from the Apple Watch.

Switch off the Apple Watch screen with Your Palm

Perhaps you have ever completed using the Apple Watch, reduced your wrist, and noticed the screen doesn't switch off? Even though it isn't an issue, and it will automatically switch off after a couple of seconds of inactivity, it'd be helpful to learn how to turn the screen off, right personally? It'd be great, particularly if you've handicapped wrist detection to save lots of battery. Well, you're in fortune, as there's a way to switch off the screen physically; and it's easier than you might think.

Once you have finished making use of your **Apple Watch** and want to turn the screen off carefully, *place your hand on the screen.* Once you move your hands away, you'll spot the screen has switched off. They have other uses too - if you receive a telephone call on your Apple Watch, place your hand over the flash to silence the Watch.

Let Siri know when you've finished talking

The usage of **Siri** on the Apple Watch makes difficult tasks like setting alarms much more straightforward to accomplish, by just telling Siri to create the alarm for you. It is also a fundamental element of the text messages app, being utilized to dictate your reply before transforming it to textual content prepared to send. But **Siri** on the Apple Watch continues to be young and has too much to learn - like when to avoid hearing your dictation.

We've discovered that when we've used Siri to dictate replies to text messages, it is not quite sure when to avoid hearing us and can begin to transcribe someone speaking near to you. However, we've discovered that tapping the flash screen after you've finished with your reply will minimize **Siri** from hearing and can transcribe what has been said.

It's not only helpful for dictation, though, as the sound clip may also be sent as a tone of voice mail via iMessage on the occasion that Siri doesn't transcribe accurately. Therefore, tapping when you've finished speaking is practical, as you do not want to send your friend a tone of **voice note** with ten seconds of silence by the end, do you?

Organize Your Apple Watch Home Screen

It's wise to organize the applications on your Apple Watch home screen. With the mixture of a little screen and a huge number of applications installed, it might become frustrating looking for apps that you would like to use.

Now, the fastest way to rearrange your Apple Watch

home flash screen is to touch and contain the application icon until it wiggles, much as with the iPhone. Once everything begins to wiggle, you can pull the icon to its new position - it's also where you can uninstall any third-party Apple Watch apps.

Additionally, there is another way to organize your Apple Watch home flash screen, namely utilizing the Apple Watch activity application on your iPhone. By starting the activity application and being able to access the App Design menu, you can get a synopsis of the design of your apps. From here, you can certainly rearrange them by tapping, keeping, and dragging them without having to be hindered by the tiny screen of the Apple Watch.

Setup the Watch on Your right Wrist (Lefties, pay attention)

Another tip is perfect for the lefties in our midst - sick and tired of wearing the Apple Watch on your left wrist? Tried it and didn't play well with the wrist-raising recognition? Don't get worried; you can change to your right wrist once you have tweaked your Apple Watch configurations in the Apple Watch partner application on your iPhone.

Once you have opened the app, navigate to *General > Watch Orientation*. From here, you can select which wrist the Apple Watch will be worn on, as well as the *Digital Crown's positioning*. By selecting the right wrist and **Digital Crown** positioning, it can help the Watch to learn when to awaken the screen as well as which way to orient the flash. Lefties have an option to make - you can either have the Digital Crown facing from your hands or use it with the medial side button above the Digital Crown. Whichever you select, it doesn't genuinely have a lot of a direct effect on your experience with the Watch.

Enable 'Prominent Haptic' for a pre-Announcement of Notifications

The decision to add a *Haptic engine* within the Apple Watch was welcomed with open arms by the tech community altogether. We've all got terrible encounters with traditional vibration motors - you've acquired your mobile phone on silent and are within an important conference when you receive textual content; however, the vibration is so noisy that each person in the area is aware you've just received a textual content. Haptic opinions aren't anything like this because of the Haptic engine, rather than feeling an enormous hype on your wrist when you obtain a notification, you'll instead feel a gentle 'tap' on the wrist to alert you. However, many people have commented that they hardly feel the haptic responses when they're on trips - *which tip is perfect for those people.*

Prominent Haptic is a pre-announcement vibration that's more powerful than the typical Apple Watch vibration to alert you of the inbound notification. To activate this, open up the Apple Watch friend application on your iPhone and get around to *'Seems & Haptics.'* From here, you can customize the noises and haptic reviews of your Apple Watch, and toggle on the 'Prominent Haptic' feature. After that, you'll feel two vibrations once you get a notification - the pre-announcement vibration, and then your notification vibration.

Answer Phone Calls on Your iPhone using the

Apple Watch

Even though we have been using the telephone feature of the Apple Watch, we missed this feature for several weeks. When you receive a call on your iPhone, you have the choice of responding to or declining the call, right?

You can find other possibilities: you have to use the Digital Crown to scroll down and gain access to them. The first option is to send an instant reply that may disconnect the decision and make available to you pre-set communications such as *"Can't speak, what's going on?"* to send to the caller.

The next option, however, is a lot more helpful; even though the telephone feature on the Apple Watch is cool, the loudspeaker isn't nearly noisy enough to have the ability to be utilized properly in a general public environment - it's just too silent to hear the call.

So, in those situations you may use the Digital Crown to scroll down and choose *'Answer on iPhone'*; this not only answers the call on your iPhone but also places the recipient on keep until you have an opportunity to get the phone from your pocket/bag and unlock it; this negates any misunderstandings on the recipient's end, as they don't hear you rustling around in your handbag looking for your telephone.

Share Your Location from the Apple Watch

There is nothing more annoying than going to a meet-up with friends and family when they keep texting you to ask where your location is - particularly when you're using an Apple Watch and can feel every text on your wrist. You have a few options here: *ignore them*, activate *Do not Disturb* setting on your Watch, or *show them where you are*. The latter appears to be the easiest option, but not when you're unsure of where you are, and that's where our last tip comes in.

All you have to do is open up the Messages application on your Apple Watch and choose a thread to answer, and rather than dictating an answer, touch the flash screen and choose *'Send Location.'* This will get your iPhone's current location and send it to everyone in the thread - which in this situation is all the friends you're off to meet. They can weight your location from within the Text messages application and easily see where you are.

Chapter 6

Apple Watch Tips & Tricks

1. Unlock Mac PC with Apple Watch

If you're wearing your Apple Watch, consider unlocking your Mac without engaging in your account password? Using PC Unlock, when you have combined your **PIN** on your Watch (and you're putting it on), your Macintosh will open without a password.

2. Add Music towards the Apple Watch

Whether it is managing downloaded music easier or streaming music directly from Apple Music plus your wrist, the Apple Watch allows it. Remember, additionally, there is currently also the state Spotify application for Apple Watch you could dive into.

Apple Music allows users to stream and focus on a couple of almost 30 million tunes, now it's on Apple Watch.

When you have an **LTE-enabled** Apple Watch Series 3,

Series 4 or Series 5, you can stream music to your heart's content. You may need a group of Bluetooth headphones.

If you're not rocking the cellular Apple Watch, you can even sync over albums and playlists and control music on your own iPhone.

3. Collection alarm or timer

The Apple Watch is, in the long run, a wristwatch - so timekeeping is rather together with the agenda. Establishing timers and alarms is easy, especially if you have Siri.

4. Use Apple Watch maps to navigate

While Google Maps is a slice from the machine, Apple Maps is a superb experience on Apple Watch - with turn-by-turn directions and local sights.

5. Best Apple Watch faces

While Apple hasn't exposed the Apple Watch towards the ravages from the third-party watch face marketplace, the quantity of choices has soared with every new iteration.

6. Update the WatchOS

Keeping your Apple Watch up-to-date means, you'll have the latest features - just like the ECG application, which launched as an over-the-air upgrade in December 2018.

7. Modular

With six complication places, the three icons underneath could be changed to common contacts to help you to help make calls straight from the Watch. It will require calendar visits and flash another engagement at heart. A company preferred.

8. Infograph

For the knowledge obsessed, the Infograph supports eight complications, just like the new corner placements; this employs the wider flash around the Series 4 and Series 5.

What's an Apple Watch Addition?

In the watch world, a complication is an added have within the watch face, as being a dial that displays the date. Apple, to be able to honor watch background, has used the terminology due to its smartwatches' widgets, which might be positioned on a wristwatch face.

They may be used to show the weather, give you news, show your battery percentage, launch applications, and more.

- **Maybe the Apple Watch waterproof?**

The Apple Watch Series 3, Series 4, and Series 5 are waterproof up to 50 meters, meaning they could survive a drop in the pool, and you don't have to take it off in the shower.

- **Maybe the Apple Watch befitting my Android?**

Android phones aren't befitting any Apple Watch. The minimal requirements are for an iPhone consumer who comes with an iPhone 5 or later dealing with at least iOS 8.2.

- **Apple Watch and Siri**

Apart from Alexa - you might have Siri on your wrist wherever you choose to go. Siri takes a large amount of work, but use our tips, and you'll take advantage of everything it offers.

The simplest way to wake Siri is to transport down the

Digital Crown - once you need to do so for just two seconds, the hearing indicator will pop-up, and you'll release.

You can also now increase your wrist towards the jaws - as well as the listening indicator should appear. Ensure it's allowed in Configurations > General > Siri > Increase to Speak.

Can the Apple Watch charge wirelessly?

The Apple Watch cannot charge wirelessly - all Apple Watch models charge through Apple's proprietary magnetic charging dock system. However, the Apple Watch doesn't officially adhere to the Qi Wireless Charging standard, as the most recent iPhones do.

How will you put Watch face towards the Apple Watch?

1. Decide on a wristwatch face that already has issues that you should edit.

2. Following that, maintain down the flash screen on your

Watch, faucet which green container you intend to edit, and utilize the Digital Crown to scroll which options you need to see your face.

3. Press the Digital Crown again to avoid wasting the complications plus your Watch face.

Will Apple Watch Monitor my Sleep?

The Apple Watch can't natively monitor sleep. Likely due to the Watch's limited battery pack life, Apple is yet to start an official rest monitoring app. However, there is a sponsor of third-party Apple Watch sleep tracking apps for the App Store that could serve the reason that you need it.

Where is the Apple Watch Battery Indicator?

Similar to methods to swipe along through iOS, WatchOS also offers you to accomplish this to get access to sure settings from the Apple Watch. If you swipe up, you'll see a share icon in the left side, below the Wi-Fi tabs, and next towards the Ping iPhone tab.

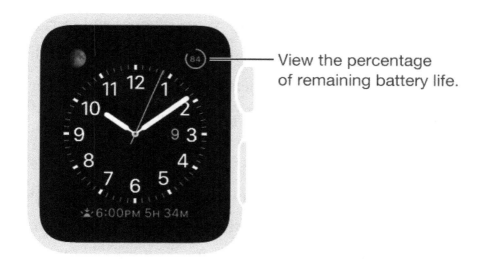

View the percentage of remaining battery life.

If you don't fancy swiping every time you desire to be sure of your battery pack, you can install the battery widget on customizable watch faces.

Discover Your apps, and Setup New Ones

Press the Digital Crown to go to a summary of all applications installed on your own Apple Watch. These symbols will contain pre-installed applications from Apple and any applications that you've on your own iPhone that will also be befitting the Apple Watch. That is clearly a choice when you set up your Watch, but if you're looking for a credit card application and can't believe that it is, or need to remove apps, then browse the

Apple Watch application on your iPhone and scroll because of the Installed Apple Watch list. Touch each substitute for discovering settings on either deleting or establishing the application form on your Watch.

To find fresh applications for your Watch, open the Apple Watch application and pick the App Store from your set of choices in the bottom from the flash screen; this would go to a version from the App Store with the apps created for your Watch, eliminating the guesswork from using the principal App Store application to find them out. The applications you install will demand the same application to become installed on your own iPhone too.

How to increase Watch Faces towards the Apple Watch?

You can include faces towards the Apple Watch by likely to the Watch application on your own iPhone and hitting the facial Gallery tab in the bottom from the flash. Here, you can select from a number of faces, which you can then personalize with problems (such as your battery pack percentage, or a shortcut to *Strava*) through the

Watch itself. You can also edit which watch encounters arrive through the My Encounters part of the app.

If you want to put something from your Photos, increase it towards the Favourites album. Once done, it'll arrive for syncing in the facial Gallery part of the app.

May I make use of Apple Pay on the Apple Watch?

Whichever Apple Watch model you have, double-tapping the medial side button, provides up your cards, and a tap from the reader lets you use Apple Payout on the unit.

Check Your Heart rate

That's easy; press the Digital Crown showing the app screen to look at the heart icon. Touch it, as well as the Watch immediately begins taking your heart rate. A graph close to the surface of the flash shows your heart rate background. Twist the Digital Crown showing other screens, wearing down your heart rate data into relaxing and walking sections.

One thing to bear in mind is usually to guarantee the Apple Watch is securely on your wrist. If it's loose, the dimension is probably not accurate.

How Apple Watch Fall Recognition Work

The Series 4 and Series 5 are both outfitted with fall detection. If it detects a hard fall, it'll hype your wrist and sound an alarm. It'll list fast usage of Emergency SOS having a swipe gesture that may contact emergency services. It'll provide a button that says "I'm OK" if you don't need help.

If the Apple Watch detects a fall and picks up you've been immobile for just one minute; it starts a 15-second countdown while tapping you around the wrist and sounding an alarm. The burglar alarm will obtain louder and louder to try and alert someone else to your requirements. It'll also automatically contact emergency services, providing what your location is.

Will the Apple Watch attach to Wireless Headphones?

The Apple Watch could use Bluetooth, allowing you to connect to wireless earphones. To do this, go directly to the 'Settings' part of the Watch, before selecting 'Bluetooth' and the unit you want to create. We've found some issues with the Watch pairing to headsets that are already proven to the iPhone, nonetheless, it offers assorted depending on which earphones we've been using.

Monitor your steps, and close the Rings

Your Apple Watch is an intensive fitness tracker. We recommend establishing Apple Health on your own iPhone to obtain the most out of the Apple Watch's fitness tracking features. Once you've, press the Digital Crown to check out the icon that appears like three rings - blue, green, and red - and tap it. The three rings represent your daily activity goals - movement (red for calorie count), exercise (green for movement), and standing (blue, using a target of standing one time per hour).

Scroll down the flash screen to find out your step count, distance walked, and the quantity of stairs climbed. The duty is usually to "close the Rings" by completing each different activity frequently. Check Apple Health on your own iPhone to get more data, or go to the Apple Watch application and choose Activity to find out even more. If you're centered on using the Apple Watch as a fitness tracker, then choose a wristwatch Face like Activity Digital or Activity Analogue to find out your progress on-screen regularly.

If you work with the Siri watch face, then your activity is shown permanently, or on encounters like Infograph, activity could be shown like a problem.

Read and Clear Notifications

When it's associated with your cellular phone, or if it's the **4G LTE** version, the Apple Watch will screen message, email, and application notifications. To learn these, you swipe down on the screen. Notifications can be found in a scrolling list, and a tap will display all the obtainable relationships. You can answer texts using quick reactions, like tweets, and use your modulation of voice instead of typing out a contact, for instance, to be sure notifications stay useful, it's good to clear out more info on them. Crystal clear them separately having a swipe left, or press and support the flash to obtain a Crystal clear All option.

Chapter 7

Apple Watch Series Best Features
Always-On, Almost Perfect

It's rather easy to go through the Watch to start out and start to see the period; I really do it subconsciously countless times every day, actually, easily don't possess an entire schedule of conferences and events. However, within an ironic twist, checking time was a very important factor Apple Watch wasn't everything ideal for - at least prior to the release from the $399 Series 5, out now; previously, the Watch's face remained dark until you raised your wrist. The Series 5's watch face is always on, so whenever I glimpse down in my wrist, whatever position it's in, I possibly could see what period it is.

It sounds just a little silly that Apple Watch is currently capable of telling you period frequently, and perhaps it really is; but alongside the heart health diagnostic tools that made the Series 4 so essential, an intrinsic compass as well as the watchOS 6 features that improve nearly every section of the Apple Watch experience. The Series

5's always-on screen makes the Apple Watch's place as the very best smartwatch you can buy.

Apple initially didn't declare a sleep-tracking feature for the Apple Watch when the Series 5 continued sale, but an unintentionally released screenshot for the Apple Watch Alarms application, shows an escape feature that was not launched. Yet, it's unclear if the characteristic will debut, and what impact it is wearing battery pack life.

Apple Watch Series 5 price and availability

The Series 5 is available to online purchase beginning with $399 (£399) for small Aluminum 40-millimeter model with Navigation; for any supplementary $100, you can splurge around the cellular-enabled watch (which also requires a regular monthly data plan from your cellular carrier for another cost). The larger 44-mm watch is $429, and $520 with LTE.

If you want a thing that looks and feels a little more high-end than aluminum, the stainless Series 5 begins at $699, and the brand new titanium model is $799. If you feel like balling out, the white ceramic special release is again for $1,299. The Series 5 replaces the Series 4, which is forgotten about obtaining through Apple but are for sale to a steal from third-party retailers. Apple is still offering the 2-year-old Series 3 for $199.

- **Screen: Always-on is a big deal**

I've used another smartwatch in industry, and most of them have always-on shows, but which means you can always begin to see the period; however, apple's version from the always-on screen is a little spare. The Series 5 doesn't merely demonstrate what period it really is. When inactive, the screen teaches you a dimmer version of most information on your watch face. I take advantage of the Infograph Modular watch face, which includes six complications combined with period; therefore I access my most-used applications (Workout and Communications) as well as components of information just like the elements and battery pack percentage. I possibly could nonetheless discover all that whenever the screen dims.

The difference is even starker with brighter watch faces like Meridian, which include an almost completely white background that dims to black when you decrease your wrist. The flash's ambient light sensor can identify how bright your environment is and change itself accordingly; therefore, the screen is never too bright or too dark.

When you're using an app, the always-on screen dims and blurs the setting showing you plenty of time when it's inactive; this concerns all of the Workout apps, which nonetheless shows all of your metrics despite the fact that you're not positively going for a go-through the watch. The only difference will be period elapsed, which refreshes every second instead of counting milliseconds; this characteristic is incredibly useful while operating because I forgot about the experienced to improve my wrist to find out my speed or time. Even in bright morning daylight, I had formed no issue viewing my stats within the darkened screen. To save lots of battery packs, you can transform the always-on part off (start the watch's Settings application and toggle it off under Screen & Lighting).

- **Compass: Maps made Better**

I'd have yawned when Apple announced that among the headlining features in Series 5, can be an integral compass; it just didn't excite me what type of FDA-cleared ECG application did when the Series 4 was announced recently. But I recognized how useful the Compass application could possibly be.

However, the compass isn't the only application that speaks good things about the watch's built-in magnetometer. Apple is starting the Compass API to third-party apps, which is also deploying it in its Maps app to permit a feature that displays for you which path you're facing. That is incredibly useful once I parked in the bottom of Runyon Canyon Car Park, and had to determine which trail to consider. Maps consistently proved to me which path I have been on, and what distance into the car park I used to be, which helped me realize when I needed to cut the hike brief and return.

I possibly could see this characteristic being a lot more essential when camping or hiking in more handy remote control areas. Thinking back to a period I acquired lost trekking in Sedona as an adolescent in the pre-smartphone region, this characteristic would've been a life-saver. (Not actually for me personally - I survived - also for someone else.)

It should be noted that one watch rings will hinder the Series 5's built-in magnetometer. Essentially, any group having a magnet in it'll toss from the compass's capacity to execute, so if you're moving out for an event, leave the Milanese Loop or Modern Buckle in the home.

- **WatchOS 6 Program Monitoring: Easy and Private**

Apple isn't reinventing the tyre with Cycle Monitoring, however, the truth that ladies can now track intervals on the very best smartwatch on industry, in addition to all or any of the other features which will make it great, is a welcome change. I've used similar features from Fitbit and Garmin, as well as the features will be the same. You'd self-report your intervals to start, and your watches will start accurately predicting when a different one begins. I'm however, in the 1st phases of using the Apple Watch's Routine Tracking app; therefore, I haven't examined out its predictions or notifications, but

I value the quantity of detail I'm able to enter when it comes to period movement, symptoms, and spotting. You can also add info regarding ovulation test results, cervical mucus quality and basal body temperature in the iPhone Health app, and invite Cycle Monitoring to predict your fertile windows if you want to utilize the application to plan or prevent carrying a child.

In the first place period-tracking, you'll have to insight your details in the *iOS Health app*, including details just like the initial day of the last period, amount of the regular and typical period length. You can begin logging your period in the *Routine Tracking application* for the watch, as well as add the application form like a problem in the watch face for easier access; I plan to maintain it being a problem within the period cycle, and swapping it out for another application.

After a Privacy International study demonstrated that popular period-tracking applications might be seeping information regarding your wellbeing and sex to companies like Facebook, Apple's on-device, hands-off approach to health data makes its version from the feature a lot more compelling.

• **Battery Life: Nightly Charging required**

We wear my Apple Watch from the time I am awakened to sort out every day 'till period I take it off to visit bed - usually around 16 hours each day. Old watches, especially the Series 3 and Series 4, could last considerably longer than that, but I never used these to monitor my sleep; therefore, i charged them each night.

The Series 5's always-on screen doesn't look like a whole lot of a power battery drain - at least significantly less than the Series 3's cellular connectivity was when that watch debuted. After a whole 14-hour daytime of placing the brand new watch through demanding actions to check, including installing apps, checking out Maps and Compass, logging my program, requesting Siri various questions, and monitoring a 3.75-mile run and a 2-mile hike as individual workouts, I have been right down to 10%, and We seldom use my watch that intensively; I've stopped charging my Apple Watch daily, and I want I really could squeak by on two times.

Rival smartwatches from Samsung (Fitbit and Garmin)

offer multi-day battery pack life, but those watches also aren't as fully presented as the Series 5; for today's time, it's yet a trade-off.

- **Design: Business as usual**

The Series 5 appears much like Series 4 in one way. Apple introduced a brand new titanium finish, which is lightweight to slide on and looks stylish personally and scale back the white ceramic edition, which really is a premium watch using a cost tag ($1,299) to check.

The classic aluminum version is still normally the one a lot of people will buy. And Apple happens to be permitting you to customize the watch finish and group before you obtain, instead of having to consider whatever comes into play the box and selecting the strap you want.

- Apple Watch Series 5 and watchOS 6: Filled up with improvements

You don't need a string 5 to get among the better new Apple Watch features. Among the major things I really like about using the Series 5, may be the latest software, watchOS 6, which is available as an over-the-air update for the Series 3 and 4, too.

The very best new features will be the new Schedule Tracking application for logging period circulation and symptoms, the Calculator app that may save relationships with an intrinsic suggestion calculator, the Noise application for monitoring decibel levels and the brand new independent Watch App Store. And that's not half from the improvements Apple shipped with this release. There's a great deal to like about watchOS 6.

I'm not amazed it took so very long to get a Calculator application to attain over the watch, due to the fact the iPad even now doesn't have an area version, but I'd never usage my iPhone's calculator again. The watch app's suggestion calculator is a God-send, especially because you can change the percentage and regulate how much every individual owes for a business dinner. When you yourself have a few drinks and neglect how exactly to do mathematics, the Apple Watch will perform the duty for you.

The Watch App Store may be probably the most apparent

gamechanger because so long as required to create watch applications from your own iPhone. Meaning app designers don't need to produce iOS applications 1st and then produce watch extensions that must get watch applications more useful and specific. I question when Apple allows Apple Watch purchasers to produce the watch lacking for just about any iPhone, too, which happens to be the biggest thing keeping the watch from being a completely impartial device.

Chapter 8

Differences between Apple Watch Series 5, Series 4 and Series 3

The Apple Watch Series 4 was announced in September 2018, but the product continues to be succeeded from the Apple Watch Series 5.

Apple Watch Series 5 smartwatch sits alongside the Apple Watch Series 3, while Series 4, Series 2, Series 1, and the original Apple Watch are discontinued.

To create things simple, we've compared the Apple Watch Series 5 to Series 4, and Series 3 here, so you can see just what the variations and similarities are, whether you want to upgrade or take the smartwatch plunge.

Apple Watch Series 5 vs. Series 4 vs. Series 3: Software

- All will run WatchOS 6

- Spare features on Series 5.

The Series 3, Series 4 and Series 5 will all run WatchOS 6 when it arrives on 19 September 2019, as well as the Series 1 and Series 2, although the program is coming later for all those devices. The original Apple Watch won't support WatchOS 5, and it'll not support WatchOS 6 either.

All generations, except the original Apple Watch, therefore all give a similar experience, even if there are numerous extra features around the Watch Series 4 and Series 5, like fall detection as well as the ECG function, as well as the Always-On Display and built-in compass within the Series 5.

With WatchOS 6, an ardent App Store, woman health tracking, improved Siri, Activity trends, and more will all be arriving on Apple's smartwatch.

Apple Watch Series 5 vs. 4 Series vs. Series 3: Models

- Series 3: Aluminium only options, two colors, Nike+ model.

- Series 4: Forget about obtainable through Apple.

- Series 5: Aluminium and stainless options (3 colors), Titanium choices (two colors), Ceramic option (one color) Nike+ models and Hermès models.

- GPS and Navigation and Cellular choices for Series 3 and Series 5.

- Size options: 38 mm/42 mm (Series 3), 40 mm/44 mm (Series 4 and 5)

When the original Apple Watch premiered, its case was obtainable in aluminum, stainless and special materials like solid platinum, which came in two size options of 38mm and 42mm. The Series 3 then launched a ceramic model, but that is discontinued when the Series 4 arrived. Ceramic is again for the Series 5, though, and also a fresh titanium option.

The Series 3 happens to be just available with an aluminium case, either silver or space grey, having a Sport Group. You can obviously buy individual straps; nevertheless, you will not be in a posture to obtain the Series 3 in stainless or any other materials.

Apple Watch Guidelines

- The Series 3 comes into play 38 mm and 42 mm size options, as well as with an array of GPS navigation simply or Navigation and Cellular. Gleam Space Gray aluminium Nike+ model available with an Anthracite and Dark Nike Sport Group. The Nike+ model can be obtainable in GPS and Navigation and Cellular choices.

- The Series 5 has a lot more possibilities compared to the Series 3, and it'll be found in 40 mm and 44 mm sizes. To begin with, there may be the typical Apple Watch Series 5, that may come in collection of three aluminium colors and nine standard Sport Group options. You will see then stainless case options, also obtainable in three colors, as well as assorted strap options from Sport Loop ring towards the Milanese Loop as well as the Leather Loop. The titanium models can be found in two color options with multiple straps, as well as the ceramic model comes into play with one color option with various strap options.

- Aluminium models can be found in Navigation and Cellular models, while stainless, titanium, ceramic, and Hermès models are Navigation and Cellular as standard. You can even use Apple's fresh Apple Watch Studio room to pair in the Series 5 model you decide on using the strap you want. Previously, you'd to get additional straps individually if you preferred a different strap from the actual model you selected was included with.

Additionally, there are Series 5 Nike+ models available, all with aluminium casings, and Series 5 Hermès models available, that have stainless casings (two colour options) and special Hermès straps. While all of the typical Series 5 models, as well as the Nike+ models can be found in both case sizes though, some of the Hermès models only can be found in either 40 mm or 44 mm, not both.

Apple Watch Series 5 vs. Series 4 vs Series 3: Hardware

- Series 3: S3 brand, W2 Wi-Fi chip, Bluetooth 4.2.

- Series 4: S4 brand, W3 wi-fi chip, electrical heart sensor, fall recognition, Bluetooth 5.0.

- Series 5: S4 brand, W3 WiFi chip, electrical heart sensor, fall recognition, built-in compass, Bluetooth 5.0

- Series 3/4/5: Barometric altimeter, ambient light sensor, built-in Navigation, optical center sensor, accelerometer, gyroscope, 802.11b/g/n 2.4 GHz Wi-Fi, 18-hour battery pack life.

- The Apple Watch Series 3 includes a dual-core brand called the S3 under its hood, together with a radio chip called the W2. The Navigation merely model has 8 GB of storage, while the Navigation and Cellular model has 16 GB of storage, as well as LTE connection. The LTE online connectivity means you can create and receive calls and texts, as well as perform all of the jobs you'd want to on your own Watch without your iPhone in range.

Both GPS and LTE and Cellular Series 3 models offer Siri directly from the watch instead of transferring it to your iPhone, because they are doing in the Series 4 and Series 5.

- The Apple Watch Series 4 and Series 5 include an upgraded brand that's claimed to become two times faster compared to the S3, called the S4. Additionally, there is another era cellular chip called the W3. Many of the hardware features will be identical to Series 3, just like the barometric altimeter, built-in Navigation, as well as the optical heart rate sensor; however, the Series 4 and Series 5 do devote several extras. They promote the accelerometer from up to 16 G-forces to up to 32

G-forces, and they also put in a power heart rate sensor towards the Digital Crown; after we pointed out, that may allow users to consider an ECG themselves. You can read more concerning this inside our independent feature. Both LTE and Navigation and Cellular models have 16GB of storage, as well as the Series 4 and 5 also offer fall recognition.

- Series 5 takes things one step further still by offering a built-in compass too, as well as international emergency calling.

Apple Watch Series 5 vs. Series 4 vs. Series 3: Design and display

- Series 3: 11.4 mm solid, 5 ATM waterproof, OLED Retina display with Pressure Touch.

- Series 4: 10.7 mm heavy, 5 ATM waterproof, LTPO OLED Retina display with Push Touch.

- Series 5: 10.7 mm dense, 5ATM waterproof, LTPO OLED Always-On Retina display with Power Touch.

- All straps compatible across all models

The Apple Watch Series 3 carries a solid rectangular body using the Digital Crown and separate button on the proper, and also a loudspeaker and mic over the left. It's water-proof up to 50-metres, and it features Ion-X cup alongside the screen. The Navigation and Cellular model is differentiated using a red accent around the Digital Crown.

The heart rate monitor is placed on the lower from the watch body, combined with release buttons for switching out the straps as well as the second-generation OLED Retina screen sits at the very top, two times brighter compared to the Series 1 at 1000nits. The Navigation model comes with an amalgamated backward, as the Navigation and Cellular model includes ceramic and sapphire crystal back too.

The Apple Watch Series 5 and Series 4 both sticks to a straightforward design and same strap mechanism as the Apple Watch models that are eliminated before them, but Apple made several adjustments with these models. To begin with, the Digital Crown on Series 4 and Series 5 models comes with an electric centre rate sensor included in it, which is usually as well as the optical cardiovascular rate sensor on the lower from the watch instances.

Apple Watch Series 5 Overview

The Series 4 and Series 5 likewise have a much bigger screen with rounded edges, making full usage of the region available and creating a bolder design. The 40 mm Series 4 and Series 5 give a 759 square meters screen area compared to the 563 square meters within the 38mm Series 3, as the 44mm Series 4 and Series 5 have a 977 sqmm2 screen area compared to the 740 sqmm2 from the 42 mm Series 3.

The bigger screen ratio makes the Series 4 and Series 5 look quite dissimilar towards the Series 3 despite the same design overall. As well as the screen increase, the Apple Watch Series 5 provides an Always-On Retina screen, which may be the primary differentiating factor between it as well as the Series 4. The Always-On screen means you don't have to increase your wrist to wake the screen up, using the display always noticeable. The raising from the wrist or a tap for the screen will brighten the Series 5 screen instead.

Apple Watch Series 5 vs. Series 4 vs. Series 3: Conclusion

If you didn't purchase the original and you've decided the Apple Watch happens to be something you want, purchasing the Series 3 on the brand new Series 5 model can help you save £200. Nevertheless, you overlook some key features plus your end choices are even more limited.

The Apple Watch Series 5 not merely adds an even more advanced brand, but it carries a much bigger screen making better usage of the problem size, an improved accelerometer, fall recognition, Bluetooth 5.0, a power heart sensor, which allows users to measure their ECG (US/UK/Europe-only for today's time), as well as an Always-On screen and an intrinsic compass.

All of those other features might stay the same, also for

some, the brand new screen design, improved processor and ECG functionality, Always-On screen, and built-in compass could be the five features you had a need to take the smartwatch plunge. For others, the Series 3 will a lot more than suffice. In circumstances of upgrades, some people that have the original Apple Watch, Series 1 or Series 2 will quickly realize some crucial distinctions by switching towards the Series 5, especially with the brand new display. Some people that have the Series 3 may also likely go to a sound difference in the brand new model. Nonetheless, it may be really worth waiting before Series 6 to learn if rest tracking turns up, or a noticeable change-up in design.

If you now have the Series 4 and you're wondering whether to upgrade towards the Series 5, you don't need to, until you want that Always-On screen function or the built-in compass.

Index

CPSIA information can be obtained
at www.ICGtesting.com
Printed in the USA
LVHW022026281220
674974LV00008B/743

9 781637 500521